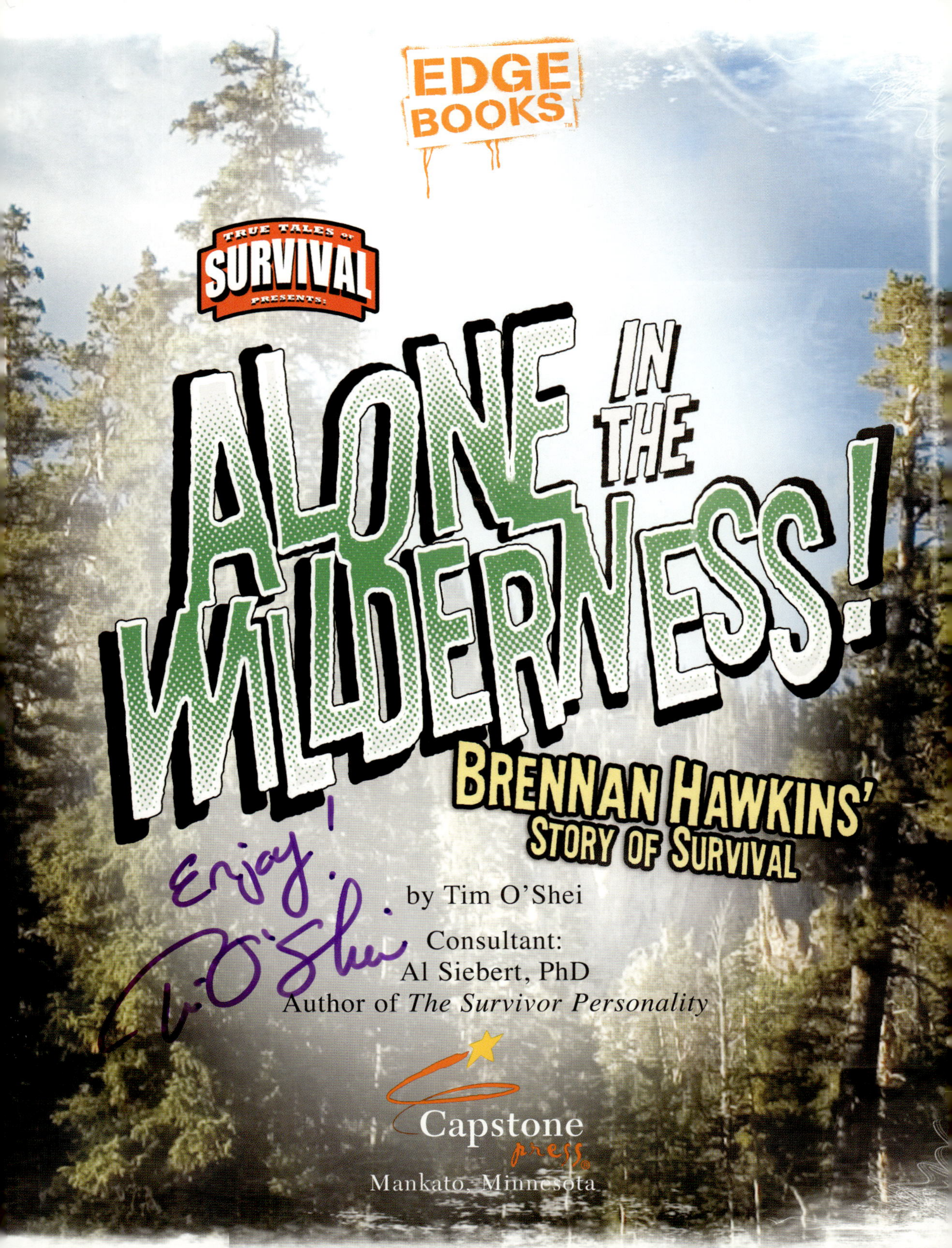

ALONE IN THE WILDERNESS!

BRENNAN HAWKINS' STORY OF SURVIVAL

by Tim O'Shei

Consultant:
Al Siebert, PhD
Author of *The Survivor Personality*

Capstone press
Mankato, Minnesota

Edge Books are published by Capstone Press,
1710 Roe Crest Drive, North Mankato, Minnesota 56003.
www.capstonepub.com

Printed in the United States of America in North Mankato, Minnesota.
012013
007146R

Library of Congress Cataloging-in-Publication Data
O'Shei, Tim.
Alone in the wilderness!: Brennan Hawkins' story of survival / by Tim O'Shei.
p. cm.—(Edge books. True tales of survival)
Summary: "Describes how 11-year-old Brennan Hawkins survived four days of being lost in the mountains"—Provided by publisher.
Includes bibliographical references and index.
ISBN-13: 978-1-4296-0087-3 (hardcover)
ISBN-10: 1-4296-0087-X (hardcover)
1. Wilderness survival—Utah—Juvenile literature. 2. Hawkins, Brennan—Juvenile literature. I. Title.
GV200.5.O84 2008
613.6'909792—dc22 2006102271

Editorial Credits

Angie Kaelberer, editor; Jason Knudson, set designer; Renée Doyle and Kyle Grenz, book designers; Charlene Deyle and Scott Thoms, photo researchers

Photo Credits

AP/Wide World Photos/Alan Murray, 26; Douglas C. Pizac, 6, 10, 13, 17, 18, 20, 23 (all foreground); Keith Johnson, 4 (foreground); Leah Hogsten, 14 (foreground); Steve C. Wilson, 27

Getty Images Inc., 24 (foreground); George Frey, 29 (foreground)

Shutterstock/Bruce Yeung, 20–21 (background); Franzelin Franz-W., 14–15 (background); Gualberto Becerra, 12–13 (background); James M. Phelps Jr., 2–3; Jim Lopes, 32; John Vanhara, 28–29 (background); Katherine Campbell, 10–11 (background); phdpsx, 1, 6–7 (background), 8–9 (background); Todd D. Nestor, 16–17 (background), 24–25 (background); Tom Hirtreiter, 4–5 (background), 18–19 (background), 22–23 (background), 30–31

TABLE OF CONTENTS

Chapter 1
LOST AND ALONE 4

Chapter 2
MISSING CAMPER 8

Chapter 3
THE SEARCH IS ON 14

Chapter 4
FOUND! 20

GLOSSARY 30
READ MORE 31
INTERNET SITES 31
INDEX 32

CHAPTER 1

LOST AND ALONE

In June 2005, 11-year-old Brennan Hawkins was on his first Boy Scout camping trip.

LEARN ABOUT:

- **A trip gone wrong**
- **Lost in the woods**
- **Thinking about family**

Brennan Hawkins trudged along a dusty trail. A thick forest surrounded him. Wind rustled the tree leaves. A river rushed nearby.

But Brennan wasn't thinking about the beauty of the trees, the breeze, or the water. He was thinking about how to find his way back to safety.

A friend had invited Brennan to a Boy Scout camp in the Uinta Mountains of Utah. More than 1,000 other people were staying at the campsite that week in June 2005. The situation seemed safe, even for an 11-year-old who had never been away from his parents.

But around dinner time on Friday, June 17, Brennan somehow disappeared. Thousands of people searched for him throughout the weekend.

Meanwhile, Brennan kept on the move. He searched for food and water. He thought often about his mother, father, brothers, and sister. Brennan was afraid he would never see them again.

Posters with Brennan's photo were put up near the camping area.

EDGE FACT

Brennan is one of five children. His brothers are Taylor, Cameron, and Mitchell. His sister is Mariah.

Chapter 2

Missing Camper

Learn About:

- Concerned parents
- No-show for dinner
- The search begins

Thick forests and clear lakes cover the Uinta Mountains.

Brennan faced his first survival challenge as soon as his life began. He was born nine weeks early. His doctors didn't expect him to live for a full day. Brennan did live, but he slipped into a coma. After two weeks, he woke up and began to recover.

PROTECTIVE FAMILY

Growing up in Bountiful, Utah, Brennan was a typical boy. He collected Pokémon cards. He was a Cub Scout. His father, Toby, took him fishing.

Brennan was excited when his friend Brian Christensen invited him to the Scout camp. Brennan's parents almost said no. They had always been protective of him. His mother, Jody, thought Brennan was less mature than other kids his age. Brennan sometimes had difficulty remembering information and relating to other people. But Brennan was thrilled about the idea of camping, and his parents didn't want to disappoint him. They decided to let him go.

Brennan was last seen near the camp's climbing wall.

BRENNAN GOES MISSING

Friday was Brennan's first day at the camp. Late in the afternoon, he and Brian went climbing on a 60-foot (18-meter) rock wall. The boys finished climbing around 5:30. Brian took off his climbing harness first and ran ahead to dinner, telling Brennan, "Catch up with me!"

But Brennan never caught up. He had taken the wrong trail. People noticed he was gone about an hour later when he didn't show up for dinner.

A group from the campsite looked for Brennan but didn't find him. It was getting late. Darkness was near. They knew Brennan could be in trouble. He was wearing only a sweatshirt, shorts, and sneakers. Luckily, the temperature was only supposed to fall to around 55 degrees Fahrenheit (13 degrees Celsius). This temperature wasn't life-threatening.

Still, he was alone. It was dark. The Bear River posed a great danger. Snow had recently melted, making the river deeper than usual. In some places, it was 15 feet (5 meters) deep. The current was swift enough to quickly sweep away a boy of Brennan's size.

THE CALL HOME

Jody Hawkins was relaxing at home when the phone rang. Someone from camp was calling to tell her Brennan was missing. "Don't waste time calling me!" Jody said. "Go find him!"

Jody dropped off Brennan's siblings with their grandmother and drove toward the camp. The ride took two hours. The whole time, Jody waited for her cell phone to ring. She expected to hear that Brennan had been found.

That call never came.

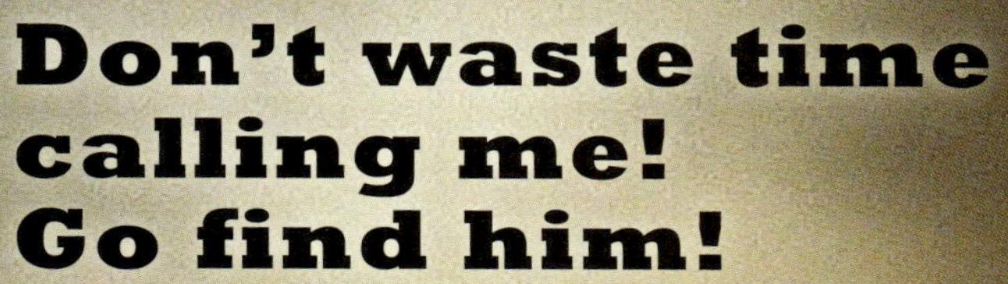

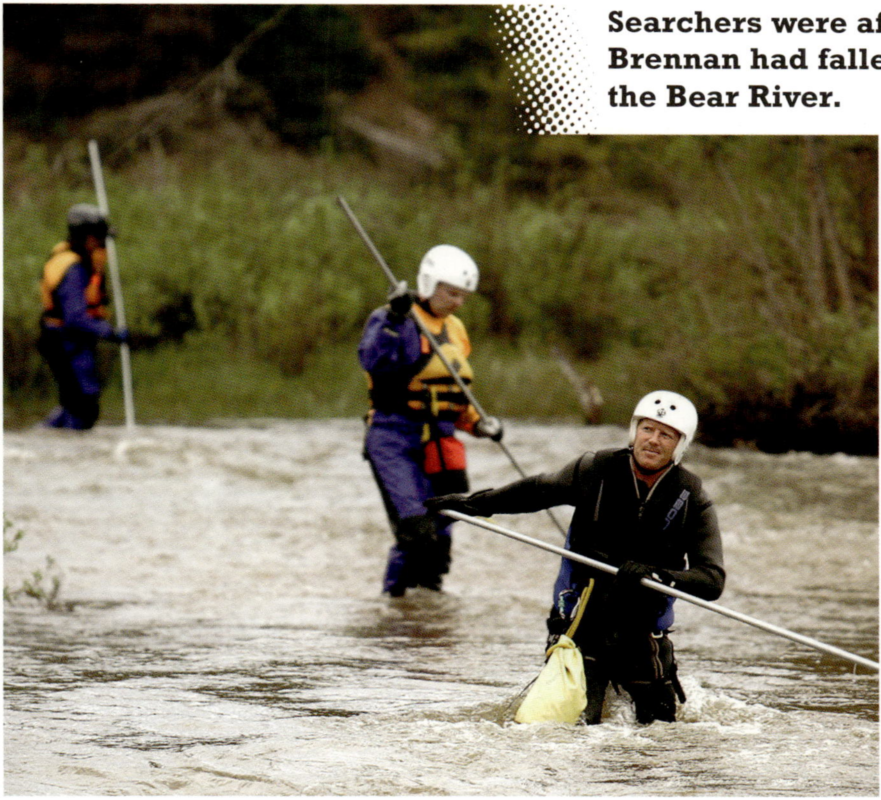

Searchers were afraid Brennan had fallen into the Bear River.

Chapter 3

The Search Is On

Learn About:

- Thousands of searchers
- Walking on and on
- Challenging conditions

A helicopter searched the woods for any sign of Brennan.

By 9:45 on Friday night, deputies from the Summit County Sheriff's Office were searching the mountain. It was dark and the Hawkins family was panicking. The campers were supervised at all times. How could one of them get lost?

The good news was that the mountain was full of searchers. By Saturday morning, at least 1,000 people were searching the mountain. Some were police officers. Others were professional searchers. Many were volunteers. All of them shared the goal of bringing Brennan back to his parents.

STAYING FOCUSED

Brennan had always been a focused boy. Whenever he had a task to do, he concentrated on it. While thousands of people searched the mountain, Brennan focused on walking. His parents had told him that if he ever got lost, he should stay on a trail. He did.

During the next two days, Brennan kept walking, hoping to find safety. As he learned later, with every step he was walking farther away from where the searchers were looking.

Brennan had no water with him. When he got thirsty, he drank from streams. The only food he had was wild mint leaves that he found.

When the temperature dropped at night, Brennan crouched down and pulled his sweatshirt over his legs. He prayed to God, asking for directions. He was scared of being kidnapped. Brennan cried until he fell asleep.

FATHER'S DAY SEARCH

Brennan's family was just as frightened. Jody wanted to join the searchers in the woods, but she was told to stay at the camp. The sheriff needed her there to tell him if any items the searchers found belonged to Brennan.

By Sunday, the number of searchers reached 3,000. Several churches in Bountiful canceled services so people could help search for Brennan. That Sunday was also Father's Day. Many dads joined Toby Hawkins in the search, explaining that if their children were lost, they would want others to do the same.

Brennan's dad, Toby, joined the search.

Many volunteers used ATVs to search the mountain trails.

Searchers found three socks and a sandal, but none of these things belonged to Brennan.

The searchers traveled the mountain by foot, on ATVs, and by horseback. The terrain was challenging. The hot sun beat down on the searchers. The wind whipped up dust, making it difficult to see. Some of the trees were only inches apart.

A team of swiftwater searchers inspected the river. They used wooden sticks and ski poles to check hard-to-reach areas in the water. The river searchers were looking for any sign of Brennan. They found three socks and a sandal, but none of these things belonged to Brennan. That was good, because the river posed the biggest danger to Brennan.

Chapter 4

FOUND!

Learn About:

- Help from friends
- Surprise on the trail
- Back to normal

The search continued on Monday with fewer volunteers.

By Monday morning, Brennan still hadn't been found. The number of searchers dropped to 600, but the sheriff promised to keep looking for Brennan. The sheriff also began investigating people on the mountain, in case Brennan had been kidnapped.

SUPPORT FROM OTHERS

One of the searchers was Kevin Bardsley, whose 12-year-old son Garrett had disappeared in the same region 10 months earlier. Garrett was never found. Kevin had promised himself that if another person ever got lost in that area, he would help in the search.

Bardsley and his wife also provided comfort to Toby and Jody Hawkins. So did many of the Hawkins' neighbors and Brennan's school friends back in Bountiful. They tied yellow ribbons along the road that led from the highway to the Hawkins family's house.

"I'M BRENNAN"

Shortly before noon on Tuesday, four searchers on horseback passed through the area around Lily Lake. They were almost 3 miles (5 kilometers) from the Scout camp. They didn't realize it, but Brennan was nearby. Brennan saw the searchers, but he didn't call to them because they were strangers.

Luckily, a man named Forrest Nunley was riding behind the searchers on an ATV. Nunley spotted a young boy who had scratches, bruises, and a bit of a rash. He asked the boy his name. "I'm Brennan," the boy answered.

Nunley gave Brennan some food and water. He noticed that the boy was wet, muddy, and shivering. Nunley gave Brennan a thermal shirt to keep him warm.

Back at camp, Jody Hawkins was asked to step into a sheriff's truck. She worried that she was going to be told Brennan was dead. But instead, she heard the good news. Brennan was alive!

Brennan was too scared to approach these riders.

After his rescue, Brennan was exhausted by his experience.

JUST IN TIME

Soon after he was rescued, Brennan was reunited with his family. He hugged his mother, father, and siblings and said, "I have the best family in the whole world." He also asked whether the Pokémon cards he had ordered a week earlier had arrived in the mail.

Brennan was taken to Primary Children's Medical Center in Salt Lake City. He had been found just in time. Doctors said that after one more night in the forest, Brennan probably would have died of hypothermia.

EDGE FACT

Searchers said Brennan's route was unusual, because he traveled uphill. Most people who are lost in the mountains go downhill.

People in Bountiful were overjoyed by the news of Brennan's rescue.

GOING HOME

On June 22, Brennan went home. He rested for a couple of days, and then life returned to normal. Only four days after being rescued, Brennan went fishing with his father and brothers.

Though people were interested in how Brennan managed to survive four days and four nights in the forest, he has said little. He has told people he doesn't recall much about his time in the woods. Even when he returned to the Scout camp with his family later that summer, he couldn't remember many details about his ordeal.

Brennan's story got national attention. Reporters wrote stories in newspapers, magazines, and online. Broadcasters told his tale on radio and television. Get-well wishes poured into the Hawkins family's home.

The Hawkins family thanked everyone who helped bring Brennan home.

Jody Hawkins kept a scrapbook of stories and letters. Meanwhile, Brennan avoided the attention. He concentrated on being a regular kid who collected cards, climbed trees, and played with friends.

People who know Brennan say his ability to focus explains why he survived. He was determined to see his family and wouldn't let anything get in the way of that goal. His strong determination helped him survive.

EDGE FACT

In 2006, the Great Salt Lake Council of the Boy Scouts had tracking devices available for Scout camps. One of these devices helped searchers find a lost scout in the Uinta Mountains.

Brennan (with his mom and sister) was ready to go back to his old life.

GLOSSARY

coma (KOH-muh)—a medical condition in which a person is unconscious, or in a deep state of sleep, for a long period of time

current (KUR-uhnt)—the movement of water in a river or an ocean

hypothermia (hye-puh-THUR-mee-uh)—a condition that can occur when a person's body temperature drops several degrees below normal

kidnap (KID-nap)—to capture a person and keep him or her as a prisoner, usually until demands are met

thermal (THUR-muhl)—something that is designed to hold in body heat

volunteer (vol-uhn-TEEHR)—a person who chooses to do work without pay

READ MORE

Boy Scouts of America. *Wilderness Survival.* Irving, Texas: Boy Scouts of America, 2001.

Norman, Tony. *Survival Skills.* Action Sports. Milwaukee: Gareth Stevens, 2006.

O'Shei, Tim. *The World's Most Amazing Survival Stories.* The World's Top Tens. Mankato, Minn.: Capstone Press, 2007.

INTERNET SITES

FactHound offers a safe, fun way to find Internet sites related to this book. All of the sites on FactHound have been researched by our staff.

Here's how:

1. Visit *www.facthound.com*
2. Choose your grade level.
3. Type in this book ID **142960087X** for age-appropriate sites. You may also browse subjects by clicking on letters, or by clicking pictures and words.
4. Click on the **Fetch It** button.

FactHound will fetch the best sites for you!

WWW.FACTHOUND.COM

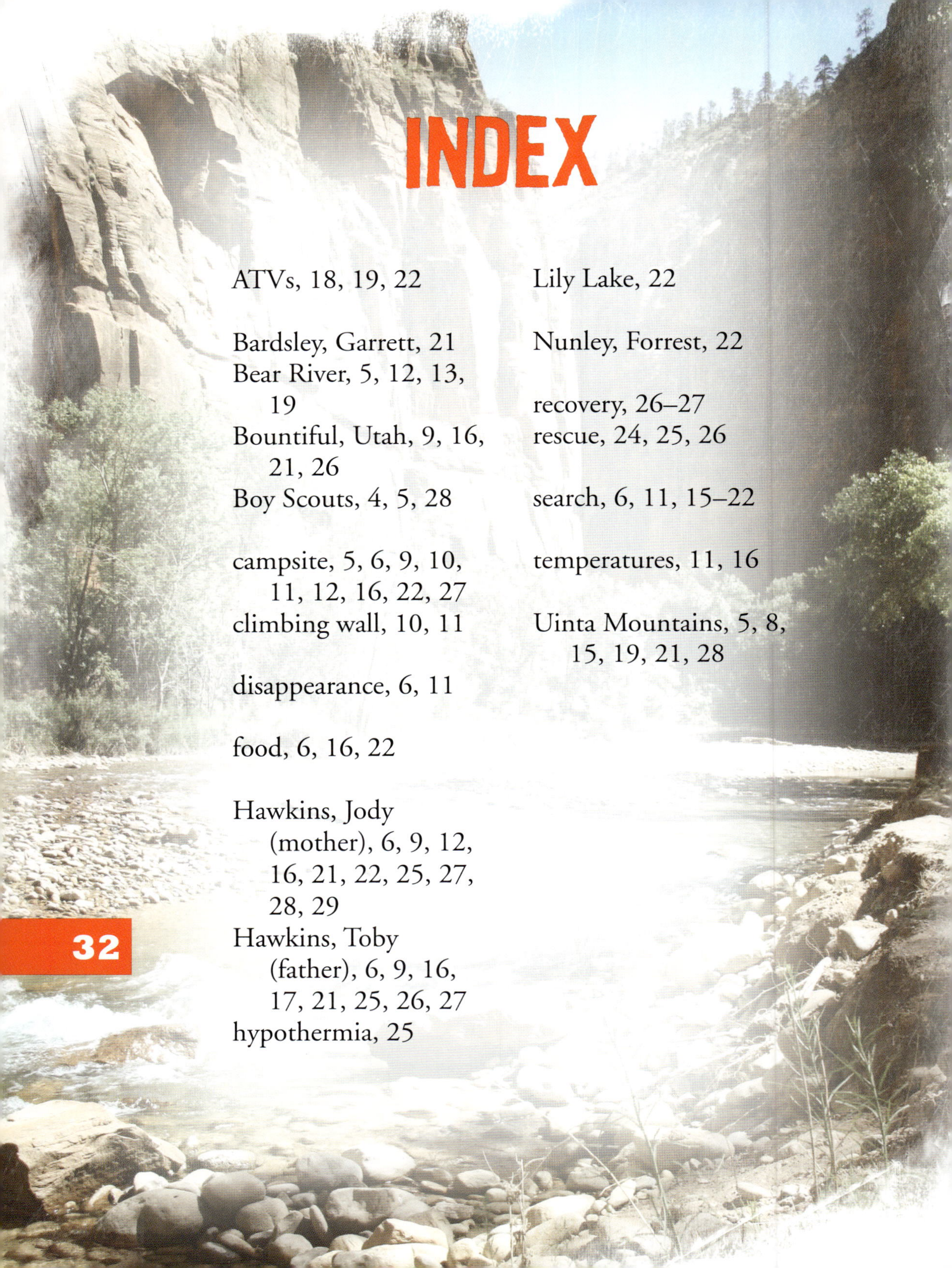

INDEX

ATVs, 18, 19, 22

Bardsley, Garrett, 21
Bear River, 5, 12, 13, 19
Bountiful, Utah, 9, 16, 21, 26
Boy Scouts, 4, 5, 28

campsite, 5, 6, 9, 10, 11, 12, 16, 22, 27
climbing wall, 10, 11

disappearance, 6, 11

food, 6, 16, 22

Hawkins, Jody (mother), 6, 9, 12, 16, 21, 22, 25, 27, 28, 29
Hawkins, Toby (father), 6, 9, 16, 17, 21, 25, 26, 27
hypothermia, 25

Lily Lake, 22

Nunley, Forrest, 22

recovery, 26–27
rescue, 24, 25, 26

search, 6, 11, 15–22

temperatures, 11, 16

Uinta Mountains, 5, 8, 15, 19, 21, 28